ADULT *Naughty*

COLORING BOOK FOR MEN

tilda mallin

Adult Naughty Coloring Book for Men

Copyright © Tilda Mallin

First published 2023

ISBN 9798374267938

Edited and typeset by Tilda Mallin

Cover design by Tilda Mallin

Thank you for showing your support. We would be very pleased
to hear from you. Please scan the QR Code to leave a review.

Amazon UK	Amazon Australia	Amazon USA

THIS BOOK BELONGS TO

COLOR TEST PAGE

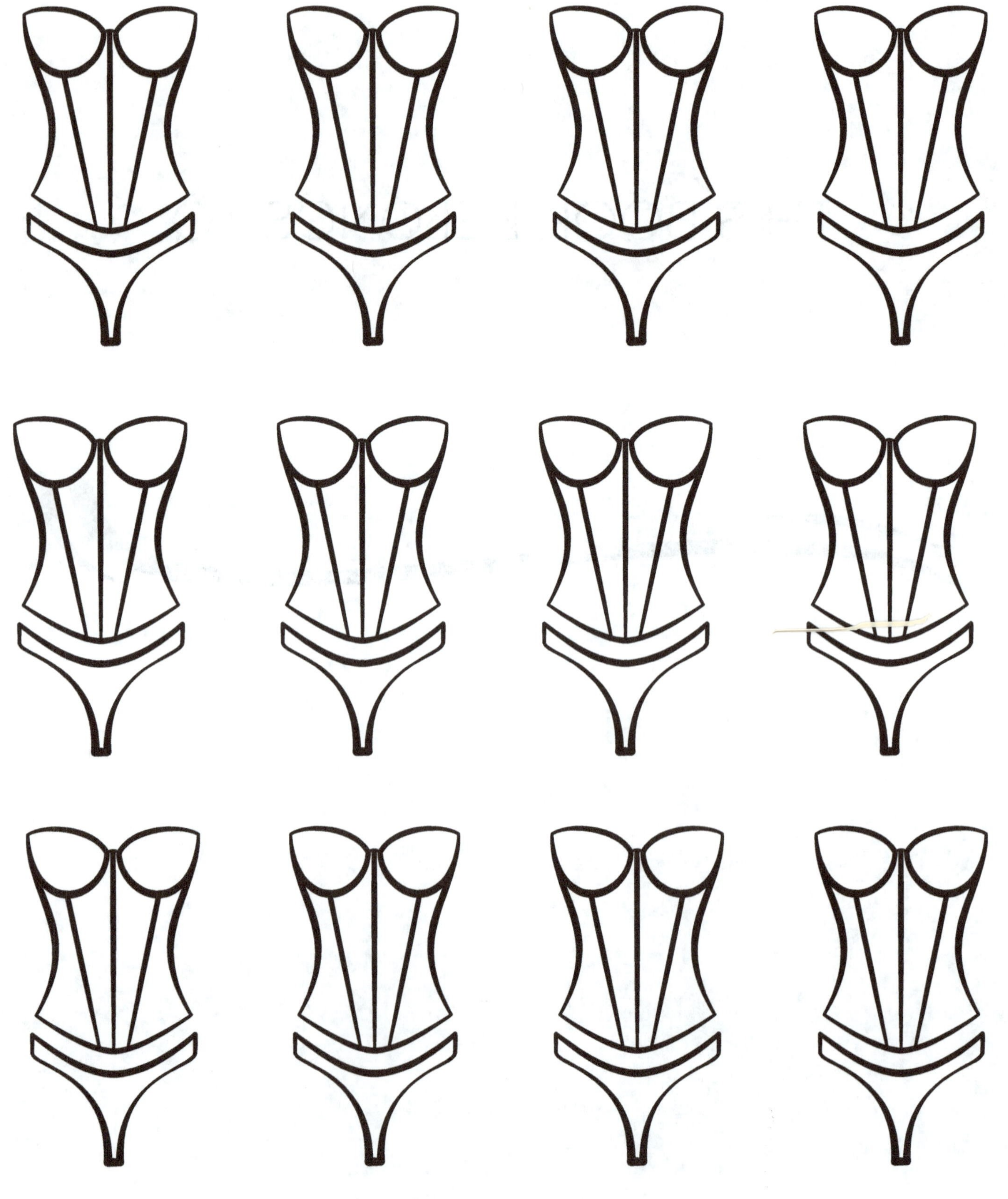

GRL
PWR

www.ingramcontent.com/pod-product-compliance
Lightning Source LLC
Chambersburg PA
CBHW080051270726
48653CB00045B/3882